A Thousand Miles of Stars

Books by Walt McDonald

Faith Is a Radical Master. Abilene Christian University Press, 2005.
A Thousand Miles of Stars. Texas Tech University Press, 2004.
Great Lonely Places of the Texas Plains. Texas Tech University Press, 2003.
Climbing the Divide. University of Notre Dame Press, 2003.
All Occasions. University of Notre Dame Press, 2000.
Whatever the Wind Delivers: Celebrating West Texas and the Near Southwest. Texas Tech University Press, 1999.
Blessings the Body Gave. Ohio State University Press, 1998.
Counting Survivors. University of Pittsburgh Press, 1995.
Where Skies Are Not Cloudy. University of North Texas Press, 1993.
All That Matters: The Texas Plains in Photographs and Poems. Texas Tech University Press, 1992.
The Digs in Escondido Canyon. Texas Tech University Press, 1991.
Night Landings. Harper & Row, 1989.
A Band of Brothers: Stories from Vietnam. Texas Tech University Press, 1989.
After the Noise of Saigon. University of Massachusetts Press, 1988.
Rafting the Brazos. University of North Texas Press, 1988.
Splitting Wood for Winter. University of North Texas Press, 1988.
The Flying Dutchman. Ohio State University Press, 1987.
Witching on Hardscrabble. Spoon River Poetry Press, 1985.
Burning the Fence. Texas Tech University Press, 1981.
Working Against Time. Calliope Press, 1981.
Anything, Anything. L'Epervier Press, 1980.
One Thing Leads to Another. Cedar Rock Press, 1978.
Caliban in Blue. Texas Tech University Press, 1976.

A Thousand Miles of Stars

WALT MCDONALD

Texas Tech University Press

This book is typeset in Bembo and Birch. The paper used in this book meets the minimum requirements of ANSI/NISO Z39.48-1992 (R1997).♾

Designed by David Timmons

Printed in the United States of America

Library of Congress Cataloging-in-Publication Data

McDonald, Walter.
A thousand miles of stars / Walt McDonald.
    p.   cm.
ISBN 0-89672-538-3 (alk. paper)
1. Texas—Poetry. I. Title.
PS3563.A2914T48 2004
811'.54—dc22

                                        2004009453

04 05 06 07 08 09 10 11 12 / 9 8 7 6 5 4 3 2 1

Texas Tech University Press
Box 41037
Lubbock, Texas 79409-1037 USA
800.832.4042
www.ttup.ttu.edu

Acknowledgments

I'm deeply grateful to the editors of the following publications in which earlier versions of these poems first appeared, some with different titles:

Adirondack Review: "Our Mother Who Taught Tumbling"
Aethlon, the Journal of Sport Literature: "Practice during the Cuban Missile Crisis," "Too Far from Town to Play Baseball"
Alaska Poetry Review: "Taking the Keys from Mother"
American Scholar: "Turning Sixty-Five on Hardscrabble"
Archipelago: "Hammering Ice to Slush," "No Wonder My Wife Is Tough"
Connecticut Review: "Sun Turns the Ice to Oil"
Descant (Canada): "Woodworker's Saturday Nights"
Drunken Boat: "Sausage in the Mess Hall," "October Compost"
Evansville Review: "Dusk at Kill Devil Hills"
First Things: "My Brother's Photos before Okinawa"
Florida Review: "Uncle Howell and the Magic of Moonlight," "Wishing for Easter All Year Long"
Gettysburg Review: "December after World War II," "Harvest," "How Much Time We're Promised," "Ranching at Glacier"
Image: "Hoping to Break the Chain"
JAMA: The Journal of the American Medical Association: "At the Bald Men's Convention," 290.14 (2003): 1827, copyright 2003 American Medical Association; "Oranges for My Sister When She Was Nine," 285:22 (2001): 2828, copyright 2001 American Medical Association; "Rattling Past Ninety," 288.1 (2002): 17, copyright 2002 American Medical Association; "When the Days Dwindle Down," 290.20 (2004): 2640. Copyright 2004 American Medical Association.
Louisiana Literature: "Jukebox Nights in Georgia"
Maryland Poetry Review: "Dawn Outside Saigon"
Michigan Quarterly Review: "Bulldozing the Outer Banks," "Mobeetee, Where Faith and Neighbors Failed"
Midwest Quarterly: "Crows at Dawn in Montana"

New Letters: "Grandmother's House at Kitty Hawk," "Some Boys Are Born to Wander"

Ontario Review: "Uncles on Sunday Battlegrounds"

Orion: "Opening the Cabin in March"

Palo Alto Review: "Anniversary Waltz"

Pearl: "Fathers and Sons"

Presbyterian Record (Canada): "In Wild Montana Mountains"

Recursive Angel: "How Aunt Martha Handled Scandal"

River Styx: "One Summer before Saigon"

Seneca Review: "Aunt Emma and the Spoils of War"

Sewanee Review: "A Little Night Music"

Southern Humanities Review: "Coat Collars Up like Thugs"

Southern Review: "A Player That Struts and Frets Onstage," "In Arnold Schwend's Saloon"

Southwestern American Literature: "Barbed Wire before Pearl Harbor"

Sulphur River Literary Review: "War Never Stops Even When All Vets Are Dead"

Tattoo Highway: "In Shallows of the Brazos"

Westview: "All Salty Summer," "Leaving the Middle Years"

William & Mary Review: "Gehenna and the County's Tires"

Windhover: "Dogs Romping until Dawn," "Parties in a Heated Hall"

Every poem in this book is fiction, freely invented, and its content comes from Walt's imagination. Any similarities between these poems and the real lives of any persons living or dead are unintended and coincidental.

Contents

Part 1: Our Mother Who Taught Tumbling

Part 2: Red Sun in the West

Part 3: Wishing for Easter All Year Long

Part 4: Hammering Ice to Slush

Part 5: When the Days Dwindle Down

PART I

Our Mother Who Taught Tumbling

Barbed Wire before Pearl Harbor

Dad rode an Appaloosa stallion, fat
as a Clydesdale, and left the fence
and posthole digger to me, the brat,
kid brother of the oldest son, the prince

who broke mustangs and played—rodeos,
cowgirls, first to ride the colt
brought back from Montana.
I never saw Tom without a moustache,

a man by the time I was born,
Mama old as a grandma,
but stern. And who could blame her,
another baby to spank by the barn

in the Texas depression. Brash,
my brother rode off at dawn with Daddy,
branding, rounding up maverick cattle
until Pearl Harbor was attacked,

when boys like my brother
rode off to war on destroyers
and never, never came back.

Our Mother Who Taught Tumbling

Mother taught tumbling in college,
coached my brothers and me to tuck and roll
before we stopped waddling, bold boys
she thought would be her fortune.

My older brothers starred in high school
but rode off to war after Pearl Harbor.
By junior high, I forgot most moves she taught.
She abandoned gyms and mats

when only one of her boys came back.
She studied nursing, changed beds
in V.A. hospitals after the war,
healed or eased whatever she could

and cleaned the rest. On double shifts
most days, she wrote letters for men
who couldn't talk, who did amazing tricks
to please her, enduring all their shots,

pulling up by the bar above the bed,
wobbling as long as they could, off balance
but breathing, before letting go and falling
off the highest beam in the world.

My Brother's Photos before Okinawa

The giggling boy in the picture is me,
riding my brother's shoulders
like a stallion with massive flanks,
unable to fall. My pudgy fists turned him,
cupping his ears like reins. Head cocked,

he looks up at the camera, lips whinnying
as if saying whenever I hold the photo,
Wasn't this fun?—taped in a scrapbook
by this pose of him in the paper
after boot camp in World War II,

my hero, local marine overseas.
More shots of him with buddies before battles,
rifle slung over his shoulder in one,
muscles where I used to ride, his prance
and big-brother whinny just for me.

Uncle Howell and the Magic of Moonlight

Out of the kingdom of wood blocks,
coyotes crouched as he carved, elk heads,
the flicker of windmill blades.

Uncle Howell made barn owls stare,
made roosters rise and crow.
The old man offered shavings to the fire

at bedtime, tossed candy we gobbled
although we'd brushed our teeth.
Shadows sprawled over goblins and lions

on the mantle, caught in the forest of Oz.
My sister swore Uncle Howell didn't whittle
but trapped rattlesnakes and hawks

and stuffed them, the fangs and beaks
too real—*Check out those beady eyes,*
she whispered, *live snakes in every room.*

But I saw him set them free from stumps
and silence in his house—Aunt Sarah dead,
the buffalo long gone, herds no one could save,

not even him, no matter how many nights
he worked with knives, how long he carved
blocks of live oak into eyes.

Oranges for My Sister When She Was Nine

I'd squeeze and squeeze until the strainer clogged,
orange pulp and seeds that filled a cup,
all for one orange juice apiece.

My sister always liked the glass
with more bubbles, foam like Daddy's beer.
Hot summer brought out her best, even in bed

with an IV dripping in her arm, her favorite scarf
knotted at her throat, loose over her bald scalp.
Always she made me sip mine first and sigh

and wipe my lips with my wrist. She licked
the rim of her glass and tipped her tongue
to the foam, leaned back and closed her eyes.

She was nine and spoiled me, a boy of five
she claimed was her nephew, not a bratty brother
like boys her friends whined about.

I never knew why. She was my favorite sister,
who died while I was in school one noon,
chewing peanut butter and bread,

sipping canned juice through a straw
until it was gone, when a teacher leaned down
and whispered I was needed at home.

Woodworker's Saturday Nights

He stained hardwood to good use
and whacked us badly, missing our legs
with the paddle when we squirmed,
and cracked our shins, our knees.
Baseballs hit that hard

would be gone, out of the park,
the seams knocked off.
Sorry was a word we never heard
unless he was drunk, or sober.
We cousins were *sorry* kids, *whack, whack.*

After dawn, by noon, we'd hear
Uncle Bob was also *sorry,* my God!
he was sorry, the war going bad,
his oldest boy captured on Bataan.
But what a carpenter, a craftsman

of cabinets in rich people's houses,
bookshelves, inlaid teakwood trays
he saved as paddles if the glue
wasn't perfect, the grain zigzagged,
something not quite right.

Coat Collars Up like Thugs

When Marva wobbled, boys parted like the sea.
Her sandals crossed like a model's
when she walked, controlled crash of hips

and blouse already thick. Marva was a marvel
of biology, classmate of skinny boys in love.
At recess, we shoved each other

off the monkey bars, defying the safety rules
and steps, climbing the slick, steep slide.
If Marva came to the playground

I don't recall. We thought she might
and that was enough for fistfights and quarrels,
knives in our pockets never opened, but almost.

She was a dish, a dimpled Shirley Temple at thirteen.
Mid-term, when Marva moved, the gang went silent.
We slouched until the recess bell and scowled

at silly first graders across the street
teasing each other on swings. Flicking cigarettes
we stole from our mothers, we trudged back

to brown steel doors, coat collars up like thugs,
checking out the fire escape, which room
it was close to, how many feet to the ground.

Gehenna and the County's Tires

Uncle Oscar burned all tires he found
until the county ruled *No pollution, no rubber fires.*
Hell was that black canyon, that stench

the devil's breath. Oscar dragged dead wolves
and antelopes off the school ground and graveyard
when he was a boy, wherever he found them,

a quarter from his father for every carcass,
habit by World War I. When Oscar came back
with a cane and Purple Heart, he found the county trashed,

abandoned cars by his fence, fenders, blown-out tires.
He hated junk, hauled tons of tires a month
and burned them. I hunted coyotes around the canyon,

hoping for bobcats and cougars. At the rim,
I dismounted and coughed, pinching my nose
and cursing. Thousands of black tires boiled,

the canyon mushy with rubber, bubbling smoke.
Coals blinked like lava, about to burst. Sometimes
coming home at dusk, I saw a glow tall as a man

beyond cactus, gone when I got there. But the horse saw.
His hind hoofs cantered sideways until I coaxed him
hard toward home, had to hold him back

when his iron shoes clattered on the highway
in shadows, ears up and sweaty, about to gallop,
the fire behind us, the cool dark barn ahead.

December after World War II

Fat weather came, a foot of snow on plains
where a dusting of snow is rare. Around town
lines snapped and big limbs broke, but nobody cared.

Dogs slid and sniffed, running with heads down,
mine sweepers following a scent. Good neighbors
waddled to the park, Jolly Jack Frost stalling cars

already old before the war. Ranches froze
like the south pole, a wonderland. How now
brown cow in the pasture, blanketed white

as a Brahma, bowing to grass you can't find.
On Broadway, old walkers ambled, faster
than they'd strolled in years, gloves flared

and cheek bones pink, waving to all
and shouting, their breaths like little clouds.
Some women hugged each Santa they passed,

happy fat men with beards, real beards that year,
who skipped on the corner, singing at all
who danced by and ringing, ringing the bells.

Aunt Emma and the Spoils of War

When she found the herd bull dead,
Aunt Emma said *Now everything makes sense.*
She accepted when the pastor was fired,
when cattle went up five cents,

when my mother's appendix burst.
Every success and death, she shook her head,
another worry bead for her rosary—
her husband's jungle rot, the long Pacific war,

the Bomb. We're thread in the eye of a needle,
she believed, beasts in a fable called fate.
I saw the grainy photograph of her as a bride
in the hall, red-lipped laughing girl

of sixteen, weeks after Pearl Harbor.
After the honeymoon, Uncle Roy shipped out.
She swore she'd die childless if he died
in combat. After the land mine

flattened him, she swore he wouldn't die.
They shipped him back, patched up and whole
except what mattered most to him.
Aunt Emma taught him the rhythm

of rocking chairs and cards, helped him
until he could ride a horse without flinching.
She talked adoption, brought the first
blind child back home in her arms

while Uncle Roy drove, tight-jawed
and tall as a stallion. For years, I watched him romp
with his kids, five orphans everyone loved—
big-grin, clumsy cousins who hugged

and clung to Uncle Roy, mellow as Emma's jam.
Aunt Emma set extra plates for my sister and me
on visits, humming, counting children like beads
and nodding, now that everything made sense.

PART 2

Red Sun in the West

Rattling Past Ninety

Fat-bellied buzzards watch
and finally take off as I swish by.
I'm nineteen, between girlfriends.

Vietnam's years away
so I'm invincible, signed up
for cadets and pilot training,

no worries about the draft.
I'm pushing eighty after a rain,
rattling past ninety in an old coupe

on a state road of chug holes,
skunk and armadillo pelts.
I mash the car to ninety-five,

past metal fatigue to a hundred.
There's a hill ahead
and I hope I'll take off,

let it come, I'm in control.
Suddenly, I'm seeing trees,
houses and red barns,

windmills, so many cattle
I'm counting, thousands
when the road curves hard

to Amarillo, and I settle back
and let it fall to sixty,
plenty of time

for the physical exam at noon,
the old car's windows down,
engine approaching hot.

Jukebox Nights in Georgia

We practiced flying with our hands—
the left, the bad guy; us, the right hand
banking to shoot him down. Nights,

we danced with local girls
while jukebox Johnny Mathis swore
we'd love until the twelfth of never,

boys who wanted wings. Songs in the fifties
were simple, country-and-western words
in any tempo, rhymed honey for the heart.

Carl and Ray and Don held on
to faithful girls back home
and married them, wearing their silver wings.

Duke walked on the moon, an Apollo marvel.
Don died in a fiery crash in Vietnam,
the youngest colonel in our class.

I've rubbed my fingers on his name
and others' on a wall in Washington
but never heard from most good friends

after jukebox nights in Georgia
when war seemed distant as the twelfth
of never, our wings only weeks away.

Practice during the Cuban Missile Crisis

Green Bay Packers worked out down there
like microbes on the snow. Earl and I
circled Lambeau Field in an Air Force jet

and watched. A mile below us, players never looked up,
nothing more urgent than block and tackle
and hit hard. For years, we cheered them on,

hard to see sometimes if the TV or Wisconsin
was snowing. On that October day, we flew there
honing our skills, dead reckoning across the North

white as the Arctic. We were boys who'd never been to war,
but dots below us were men, x's and o's on a gridiron
like a battlefield. Down there were end zones

where Bart Starr often threw bombs, the Ice Bowl
in four more years where Dallas Cowboys would freeze.
That month, we didn't know there'd be Super Bowls

someday, didn't know if there'd be another game,
if today was our last flight before missiles.
After watching men charge and fall back,

charge and knock each other down, we banked
and headed back to Truax Field at Madison,
full power and climbing, and red sun in the west.

One Summer before Saigon

That August, I came with Ursula to the tomb,
ducking under marble archways to the wall.
Ivy tangled down, coiled like snakes
chasing their tails. Blonde Ursula
without a bra, silk blouse unbuttoned
to the breast bone—what would Uncle Joe
have said to that? Say *Holy nipples, girl,*

say *Hug old Uncle Joe.* That year,
I defied Aunt Peggy's frown, *Behold,
the hussy comes.* Childless, Uncle Joe
had left me his ranch, his Purple Heart
and Silver Star, his cattle and stallions.
And so that morning after communion, I took her
to the tomb for Uncle Joe's amusement,

knowing Aunt Peggy would sneer and scoff
inside pink marble, would have boxed his cheeks
with both big-diamonded fists, *Down, you lecher,
down!* She'd know we had come from church
where Ursula gave sweet tongue to the bishop,
who balked and laid the wafer there—
that naked tongue, tight blouse confessing flesh.

All that, one crazy summer before Saigon,
the savage meat I needed. Before port call
and the long flight overseas, I spent
last nights in a bedroll, as far from war
as cattle in pastures of coyotes,
calm in the dark by my campfire
under the hottest stars there are.

Dawn Outside Saigon

We heard swans lift off at dawn,
flutter of wings after battle.
Nights, we crouched in bunkers
or cursed our luck and prayed,
cracking knuckles like beads,
sirens wailing in Asian skies

Here there be rockets.
So why not tons of sand above us,
sandbags stacked on logs
dragged out of jungles,
like storm cellars dug for homes
ten million miles away,

not enough dirt in Asia
to stop rockets launched in skies
zigzagged by choppers' shrill
staccato fire and red lights
flashing, *whop-whopping* fast,
hunting for someone to kill.

Too Far from Town to Play Baseball

In the heat, we played seething slow-pitch
with the Air Police, who bumped
and leaned to cleat us when they could.
Oh, how they hated wimps in Vietnam
who flew, who packed no weapons
but ordnance other enlisted loaded.

Our field was short and monsoon soggy,
surrounded by jungle two hundred feet
from home plate, and so baseballs were banned.
Scuffed softballs were kid stuff
even to us, so everyone swung hard
like bashing skulls. Bombs we dropped

stopped nothing, the Ho Chi Minh Trail
no wider than a baseball diamond, cargo
always moving down from Hanoi docks.
I don't know how many Vietcong died.
Between flights, we battered balls
but seldom reached the trees.

Most Air Police were hairy and six-two.
Like us, they hated to lose. We cleated
and knocked each other down on the base paths,
picked fistfights on called strike-three,
especially when it was almost dark
with runners on, bottom of the ninth.

Sausage in the Mess Hall

Nights, my skiff stalls in the fog
until I swing legs down and wade ashore,
disgusted. At dawn, black coffee

to drown the dreams. No keg of beer
for breakfast—this is yellow Texas sun
like eggs over easy, not Vietnam.

Songs of daily bread belong to finches
giddy in the sycamore, feeder packed
with pounds of sunflower seed.

I'm back at my fighting weight. On the deck,
I'd rather sing than eat, no arias of ham
and grits, thick bacon or imported cheese.

Doves coo like slow maple syrup
over Willie Nelson's twang on the radio.
Rocket attacks came back last night,

crackling like static from Saigon.
In the shower, I throw my head back
and shout old bawdy squadron songs,

no one to stop me. I try to wash it
down the drain, memories of sausage
in the mess hall after the night's attack,

more bodies in the morgue, somebody
splattering catsup over eggs and steak,
pumping up for battle, hot food to die for,

Billy Joe and the Outlaws blasting songs
on the jukebox, fat cooks shouting
and big lids slamming down.

Anniversary Waltz

On the stairs, near the top of the stairs,
she waited like a sweetheart in a cheap
soap-opera scene, and me the maverick come back.
Ursula played the heiress beset by every suntanned Tad
and Biff mad for a looker like her in scenes like that.

That day it might have been Biff or Lance
with a shiny tie, holding a program for her
at the opera in Austin, already distant from him
and focused on me, wild for her amazing lipstick
and hair, yes, and her tiny waist in that black dress.

What was a pilot in town for the weekend to do
after she had gone off to college and me half-mad
to Saigon, dog-fighting day and night
in bars and foreign skies? I attacked
two stairs at a time, always the clown, half-Joseph,

half-Romeo to her one of a kind—*Behold,*
my leap and shuffle said, *this dreamer comes.*
And she, blue-eyed and dazzling, unhooked and tugged
at her left glove, then let me take her hand,
both hands, and it was true, she had no ring.

After giddy hellos and hugs, after the opera started
and the lobby cleared and it was obvious
even to ushers she was the mother-to-be
of our children—grimly, digging for cigarettes,
Biff or Lance went down the stairs.

War Never Stops Even When All Vets Are Dead

The fields are calm tonight, not one wild coyote howling.
The windmill's still, not creaking, no restless billy goats
banging against the fence. How many nights
have we been like this since our children were born?
I imagine the ticking of Grandfather's clock,
the far-off barking of dogs, the pack maddened by blood,

the whir and clatter of the roof in blizzards.
Talk takes me back to a war years ago, most records closed,
engraved on stones in towns around the states.
I think of Harper and Don, names on a wall in Washington.
I picture children, some missing arms and eyes
outside Saigon, shells exploding decades later

in fields turned into schools, playgrounds surrounded
by jungle growing back, the sudden burst and smoke.
Then I sit up and go to the glass and look out,
knowing I'll see the moon and silhouettes
of trees, not soldiers crouching through shadows,
not fire or smoke, or children bleeding.

No Wonder My Wife Is Tough

Da Vinci carved hands like that, but fists
of this family? Curved vessels bulge
under skin like thinnest leather,
hands relaxed but powerful,

enough muscle to feed the knuckles blood,
and not an ounce of fat. Not a blotch,
not one age spot on women of fifty.
My wife carves lamb and hands the platter

to a double cousin who's come back.
I never met him in Saigon or later, until today.
Like her brothers, her cousin is huge,
ducks under the door frame, a giant

by his mother and Sicilian wife.
No wonder Ursula is tough, that our boys
are bigger than me, our daughters beautiful
and bold. Her cousin's children play

outside with ours, his eight adopted
from different landscapes, some scarred
with skin grafts. Some hobble on plastic legs,
one without arms. Her cousin could grab my skull

like a softball, man who digs up steel
around the world, who hunts down bombs and mines,
turns killing fields to farms. Her brothers ranch,
donating beef to the town's food bank.

Often, they clutch me by the arms and scuffle,
horseplay like one of their own—their massive hands,
in spite of gloves, like cactus with all the thorns
rubbed off, their hard-boned faces bronze.

PART 3

Wishing for Easter All Year Long

Dogs Romping until Dawn

After going to the wall last fall, I'm vicious with easy rage
and prayer. Puzzled between guffaw and *What?* I pause,
claws springing open to defend whatever of me remains.
Always there are skulls to bash, hearts to cut out,
and mine seems likely. After Saigon, I'm wary

of ambush, nicked machete ready to hack bamboo away.
The neighbors' house cats hiss when I jog by,
crouch and slither inside carports, behind cars.
They've seen that look on cougars lolling by caves—
I've never been one for mercy, so watch it.

I might jack the widow's tire to fix her flat,
smoke peace pipes with bullies I beat up in school.
I give myself away in *please* and *thanks,* no matter
who snarls back. I hang on every word my wife
or desperate neighbor says. I listen hard,

not interrupting, slapping my arrogant tongue
with a tire iron tucked under my belt. I turn the compost
that glows in the dark like phosphorous, gardens
for the town's food bank. Often, I hear the back gate click
and find some buddy with a grudge, in trouble with the law

that says *Forget.* He brings his St. Bernard
and our dogs romp until dawn while we sit
picking off weeds with our fingers, telling each other lies,
surprised we can laugh in the dark in a garden,
how steady our aim, how easy it is, now, not to kill.

Harvest

Nine bulls out of ten were a waste,
no fatted calves, no pedigrees.
We made them steers and fed them

to meat counters, months
after lazy alfalfa pastures.
Without a calendar or cows,

steers in shade by the pond
had thought all this was theirs forever,
grain in the troughs, and salt blocks.

Artists of the cud and tongue,
they carved delicious marble
and waddled off to wade and lap the lake,

tails flicking at pesky flies,
not bothered by wind or showers,
the shout of cowboys by the corral,

the final blast of air brakes,
trucks from the slaughterhouse
backed tight to loading docks.

Mobeetee, Where Faith and Neighbors Failed

There's nothing here but widows
and a dozen bachelors inside the boundaries
town signs claim. The average age is eighty,
clerks and ranchers hobbling along on oil wells

or victory gardens and food stamps.
My great-greats moved here with Quakers in 1880,
seeking peace at the top of Texas, before most,
disgusted, rolled covered wagons to the Gulf.

Leaving Ohio farms, they bartered land
from Comanches for Bibles and a bony cow,
a steal like Manhattan Island. It says
Mobeetee on the map, the puzzling word

they heard breech-cloth Comanches say.
Smooth-chested natives never smiled,
saying it slowly to their faces, *mo-bee-tee*
—buffalo dung, the runny kind, not chips

women gathered in baskets and burned.
These flat plains seldom rained, crops failed,
and wind blew down the tents. Years ago,
I found stone walls of a house they abandoned

after drought and more dead babies, after cowboys
told Great-granddaddy what *mobeetee* meant.
One turned his head to spit from his stallion,
not even smiling as they trotted off.

Here are his first wife's stone, and his.
Great-grandmama let them stay,
but had herself brought back and interred with him,
today, believing in words, *one flesh.*

How Aunt Martha Handled Scandal

When Uncle Dan called from the drunk tank,
Aunt Martha toppled over, sobbing,
tugging five generations of family talents down

like vases crushed under marble arches,
the whole, wide coliseum of pride.
How dare he call her, days before the divorce?

Enough to be caught with a harlot
in the town's fountain, moon bathing and rude
to the constable, fondling a marble Venus

her father shipped for the plaza after Sicily fell.
If the Colonel could see his son-in-law now,
caught by a photographer atop the statue,

making a mockery of art. Aunt Martha's lawyers
fixed it, of course, and the photo vanished.
The paper ran a mug shot of a lovely toddler

and her dog. Aunt Martha donated more
rose gardens, had glass walls installed
in the plaza, bulletproof, around the statue,

the same protection as the *Pieta,*
assuring no brute would ever touch
that face again, those perfect breasts.

How Much Time We're Promised

Suppose a truck backs over you
in your alley, its warning horn
not working as you lift the lid

of the Dumpster to toss a trash bag in.
That's how my neighbor Bobby said
the heart attack hit Fred. Built like a bulldog,

Fred was a plumber five doors down,
a check-up only last month. Big Fred
won Golden Gloves in high school,

nose broken twice, five kids and a wife.
I heard the siren at dawn like a gong
under water. Out of the shower,

dried off, I saw nothing by the curb
through the curtains, sat down for coffee
and heard a knock, and it was Bobby—

for Fred was gone, maybe dead
before his face hit the floor
and his dropped coffee splashed.

Fathers and Sons

Roundup lasted a month, ten miles of ranch
without a stray, Cora Belle in town
with her mama, sewing her trousseau.
Trousseau, a word Carl heard

when he fought in France. 1921, good luck
for a cowboy back from World War I,
too poor for chaps, wearing his army leggings
against rattlers and cactus. *La belle,*

my father must have thought when he saw her
after the war and jerked his horse to a stop,
c'est la vie, oui, oui. Home with only a limp
and a horse, our dad fought drought and the bottle,

saving his pay for a buggy and shack
by the bunkhouse. On their wedding day
he rubbed and fed his horse, bathed in the tank
and lathered, shaved smooth as the day

in 1918 when he mustered out.
In World War II, our Angus herds
fed an army, thousands of steers
and our own long slaughterhouse,

but my oldest brother died on Okinawa
in 1945. The day I left for Vietnam,
I brushed Dad's thinning hair in the hospital,
flat on his back, unable to talk, his big fist

gripping the bed rail like a claw.
Even now, at sundown on the plains
I think of Dad staring west from his gelding
at an island thousands of miles away.

October Compost

Fall hauls us to the dump
and plows the plunder under,
corners of our backyard steamy,

compost of leaves and lettuce,
peach halves the old dogs gnawed.
We toss whatever's ripe for silage—

coleslaw, okra and squash
too long after harvest, tomatoes
soft as English sausage. Chop,

stir it in, vegetable shepherd's pie,
leaves layered like a flaky crust.
Now let the dark pot boil, autumn sun

turned down, continual simmer
into December, nights chilly enough
for fire, children long gone,

scattered like pollen, skin of our arms
and knuckles shriveled. On the sofa,
we lean and hold each other's hands

and watch flames leap and flicker.
Logs in the hearth break apart by midnight,
orange embers holding heat like fists.

Uncles on Sunday Battlegrounds

Old boys, gone off alone down range,
I miss your sweaty arrogance and bluff
about Pearl Harbor when most of you
weren't twenty. Stiff necked and grumpy,
you would have died for all of us at Midway,

Normandy, battles I wouldn't have heard of
except for you, who fought and came back
gaunt and giddy or weary, bitter and lame
as years went by, nothing ahead but scandals
and politics in a country gone to the dogs,

parking lots crammed with foreign-made cars,
Okinawa, where buddies died, given back to Japan.
Sunday afternoons were uncles who argued
and smoked cigars, a rut of politics in fall,
old bulls butting each other off with sarcasm

they called logic. They were never off balance
for long. Loud out-shouted whoever talked. Outside,
after potluck tables that sagged like belted bellies,
after seconds of cakes or cobblers, the battles raged,
smirks and sneers but never fists. Pachyderm

or mule, it didn't matter—all snorted or brayed
their cousins and bureaucrats to scorn.
Old soldiers shook gray heads and lowered cigars
like horns and scoffed, flicked inch-long
sagging ashes and watched them fall.

Wishing for Easter All Year Long

Spring, and a blizzard howls a mile away.
A blue, bug-hungry jay attacks the walls—
hop, hop—hits the planks like a toddler
and pecks the wood worms out.
Ursula may think I'm playing darts.

I hope she rolls, goes back to sleep an hour,
for all's quiet, now. The jay flies up
to the feeder, gobble gobble, swallow.
We've come three thousand miles
to climb steep slopes and stare,

too far from grandchildren and friends.
At dawn, like a monk, I say the names
I know on the wall in Washington.
I wish for Easter all year long.
I don't hear rockets or gunfire, now,

but I feel glass rattle behind me,
jet bomber high above clouds. God,
let blizzards howl, let peaks turn white.
Let elk climb steeper slopes for weeds,
let cougars come, whatever we can't stop.

PART 4

Hammering Ice to Slush

Hammering Ice to Slush

Wind flings snow over stalks like cobblestones.
Cattle wait out the storm in windbreaks
far from barns. They know when it's over
we'll drive out on tractors, hauling hay
and hard alfalfa pellets. They fear no evil,
since every dawn we come and hammer ice to slush.

Nights, we rock on the deck and watch the dark.
Children we raised are safe in cities lit
by a billion kilowatts. We know spring runoff
will water summer's hay, we'll own the ranch
someday, if luck and hard work save us,
knowing these dusty plains are home,
our south and north, a thousand miles of stars.

Hoping to Break the Chain

My cousin lifted his foot to a chair, and it broke,
toppling him like a fat man in a hammock,
the chair mashed flat. His sister leaned on the wall,
a popping of unstoppable laughter and staccato hiccups.
Always they fought over nothing, but laughs
were reason enough for murder, said the frown

in my cousin's fist. I remember they rolled
and scuffled on the floor while I stood posted
at the door as a lookout, or merely stared,
the kid who couldn't tell, couldn't break them up
or make them leave me alone. Someone had to pay,
the wrath and stagger in our uncle's belt

turning us all to drink. Now, at bedtime, when I'm alone
with my wife, I wonder if our children's children
are in their parents' arms, kissing goodnight,
tucked in and calling across the room those lullabies
and psalms we taught our children, the grace
of bedtime laughter, the simple blessing of names.

Grandmother's House at Kitty Hawk

No one old strolls by. Wind blows
and tides roll wide across the dunes.
Miles of condos dare the hurricanes,
homes that tumble down like sand.
Couples holding hands hike by, widows,
families with dogs. Puff clouds

miles away could be gunfire, and were
when gray U-Boats sank freighters in 1942.
As a boy in World War II, I skipped flat rocks
on ponds, nothing else for boys to do,
big brothers shipping out, mothers
biting their lips, some fathers looking off

and coughing. Out past the Outer Banks,
four centuries of ships went down, hundreds
of masts and hulls reduced to scuba brochures.
And still they sink, trawlers hull-deep
in troughs, freighters from Singapore
and Spain, trusting lighthouse and sonar.

Grandfather fished for flounder, croaker, drum,
his beachfront house no bigger than the shack
the Wright boys hung their hammocks in at Kitty Hawk.
Grandmother heard a clatter of pistons, but guessed
it was only their glider crashing again
and didn't watch. She huddled at night in the cold,

December wind so loud she heard the devil at the door,
ripping the roof. Storms made her fear flying
forever. She grieved for me in pilot training,
hanging a Gold Star already in her heart.
She believed I'd crash, cursed wild Ohio boys
who tinkered with wings and rudders, nothing safe

at Kill Devil Hills, not even the ocean
Grandfather fished, his rod bent double with mullet,
supper for children forever hungry. All year,
he brought home oysters and sea trout, conchs
and starfish as toys, until the sudden December storm
when his trawler and a dozen other boats went down.

Dusk at Kill Devil Hills

Our son flew an Army gunship here,
big rotors pounding, training
for battles in Bosnia so far away
the chopper's guns stunned no one.

On sand packed hard,
I bend to take a mollusk
carved like scrimshaw,
like shells our son sent home.

On a windy day like this,
the Wright brothers flew the dunes,
marked now by a pylon, checkpoint
our son's crew used to turn back

to the post. Seagulls glide and bow
to whatever grace waves spread
across the sand like cards.
Whitewater splashes, churning salt

to foam. Beyond the breakers,
dolphins leap like dark Crayola arches
our granddaughter draws at his desk.
Beasts loll beyond the Outer Banks,

teeth shockingly white in the dark
where scuba divers with lights
confound the sharks, the rock fish.
Already in Bosnia it's dark.

We've followed him this far
to watch the dolphins, the dunes
near Kitty Hawk, the skies
where our boy trained. Tonight,

his crew flies over snow fields
thousands of miles from home,
watching for gunfire and rockets,
aiming their starlight scope.

Bulldozing the Outer Banks

Surf pounds the Outer Banks
and siphons tons of sand each night,
eroding maps we've drawn
of what the east coast means.

No landmark stays the same,
even silhouettes on maps
of animals we fancy—Nag's Head,
Fetlock, Parrot's Beak.

We stack fat concrete slabs
like building blocks, pile drive
steel piers for condos and hotels,
but water knocks them down,

floods docks and beach-front condos,
inlets, even Kitty Hawk.
The tide shifts sand like assets
in Swiss banks, and sand

ends up in Georgia, Scotland,
who knows where. Like children, we haul
and stabilize the sand, and drag
lighthouses back from beaches

that ebb like playtime days
we wished could last forever,
when one by one at dusk
our mothers called us home.

All Salty Summer

Someday, when grandchildren
flip through family albums and find
these brittle photos of the coast,
the weeks they ran to us
and giggled in the surf,
will they remember?

Hoard, work fingers to the bone,
give heart and dollars
to all good causes that knock,
it doesn't matter: this conch
washed up and hollow as a heart
is ours, for now.

If all our heartstrings snap,
flapping in the gale-force sugar
of good deeds, and we're old,
picking up pennies spilled
from a thousand alms,
it doesn't matter. Give,

if we wish, just do.
The tomb takes care of time.
On a peaceful beach one year,
grandchildren danced and called us
Mamaw and *Pop* all salty summer,
sweeter than ice cream on a stick.

Parties in a Heated Hall

By autumn, the heart beats
hollow as an eight-foot drum
that takes two boys to pound.

They take turns swinging, *Boom,*
and staggering. A marching band,
three hundred strong, can't drown

the bass drum out. Boys beat it hard
and nearby hats bounce off,
the home team behind at the half.

Leaving sixty is no season
for marching bands and drums,
but piccolos in a heated hall,

Guy Lombardo saxophones
for waltzes, grandmothers in gowns
and beaux in party hats.

Ring out the old and throw confetti
wildly with the throng, a night
of Times Square madness

before it's time for indoor rockers
and oxygen for the heart,
at most a few more months of ice.

A Little Night Music

If Mozart watched willows in storms,
he saw concerto chords—not trunks and leaves
but songs, sheet music in the air, the highest C
and frenzy of violin lightning, then calm adagio
after gusts, branches like French horns relaxed.

When bats flew by, he'd see allegros of wings
zigzagging after gnats. All squalls were sonatas,
vivid and finished, easy to transcribe,
overtones already there, like the clash of bat snouts
sniffing fizzing mosquitoes, the elegant

glissando of barn owls diving after mice.
Why bother jotting that down? Who in Vienna
could tell a genius from a copy boy?
Who else detected melodies from bats,
heard wings in that dimension,

harmonics odd but clear as bird songs
in his ears? Others would take the easy way
someday and scribble the obvious,
pretend raw dissonance is modern,
and some rich emperor, tone deaf,

would call that chaos *opera*. Anyone could hear
staccato in the wings of hummingbirds,
discern irregular cadence, eighth notes
of bouncing butterflies. *But musical bats?*
they'd say. *My God! Mozart, you're mad.*

Taking the Keys from Mother

She won't let go, those keys are hers,
paid for, the car her only way away.
Gray as a stranger, our mother hates us,
teeth gritted hard as her car wedged tight
against the house. My sister wants to faint,

turns away, squeezing a plump wing chair
like an accordion's sad song,
Make the world go away. My brother's hand
looks massive on Mama's lap, around her fist.
On his knees, he won't let go,

no matter how hard she jerks
to keep the keys, how fiercely she hits
and kicks. Sometimes the mind can't answer
why hands turned the wheel too late,
tires bouncing into somebody's house.

It took a wrecker to free the car again,
to haul it off. Five wrecks, each time
the last, we decided, but next day
she was rational, clear eyed and sorry,
and one of us buckled and the alliance broke.

Now, how to take keys from Mama's fist
and expect kisses? We all swear fiercely
in whispers we'll take turns driving her
gladly day or night, anywhere, always,
but Mama, please, it's time.

In Shallows of the Brazos

We taught our children to swim, swing out on ropes
and jump, trusting oak limbs to hold them
and then let go, the Brazos muddy enough to walk on.

Home was our children, cattle and cactus, our parents
who left heirlooms and Grandfather's ranch.
Decades went by like the Brazos, river of the arms of God.

After chemo, I stripped to my trunks on a sandbar.
Lay down by my wife in the shallows, on sand
sinking slowly beneath us. Reached often

and touched her, eyes closed, enough to be close
after sixty. Felt water lapping my neck, my ears,
the river a big cat sniffing and licking,

saving the best for last. Years ago, our children
all walked away without beds, picking up
where their parents began before children

when we lay back in the shallows exhausted,
outrageously young and blessed, eyes closed
on Grandfather's ranch on the Brazos,

enough to touch hands in the river and listen,
our ears underwater, long after war
without cancer, no madness anywhere.

At the Bald Men's Convention

Weeks after chemo, I stop by
as a guest. *Just browsing,* I bow,
not certain I'll be back.

Smoke fills the room, rings
wobbling over brows like laurels.
Doctors swear my slick, bald pate

won't last, like a lick-and-stick
tattoo in school. So I feel
out of place, back in sixth grade,

touch-football locker rooms
with other hairless boys.
Most chrome domes here are bald

and proud of it, biting black cigars.
They strut as if they've traded hair
for wealth. Backs of most scalps

wrinkle down like icing
sagging on hot, lop-sided cakes.
My eyes bounce off bald heads,

wondering Did a razor blade do that,
your mama's DNA, or chemo
like mine? I'm rubbing my skull,

feeling skin for stubble,
like checking for signs from the coach
when I stood safe on third

and the next batter was up—
Is it bunt, steal home,
be ready for a sacrifice?

Turning Sixty-Five on Hardscrabble

More, the body roars, the heart begs *more,*
the only adjective worth saving. Muscles sag
no matter how many hours a week I jog.

I can't stop hiking canyons to see what's west.
My fingers fumble turning the calendar—Do this
and this today, and what's for tomorrow?

Our home's a clutter of clocks and bowls,
craft and carpentry hobbies. I'm thumbnails
cracked and brittle, spotted black by hammers,

no end of wishing, growing always out
and old. I'm bald, but hairs like grass
sprout from my ears and back. Drought

hangs on all summer and pastures burn.
If readiness is all, my old bones boast,
I'm here. Trees wilt, and wild flowers limp along.

All life is grass, our hot steers snort,
chewing their endless cud. Pull Bermuda grass
from flower beds, lay plastic down,

but still the sprouts grow back,
a tangle of tough albino roots, like fish
in caverns underground, eyeless but alive.

PART 5

When the Days Dwindle Down

Some Boys Are Born to Wander

From Florida our son writes, *How many elk?*
How many big horn sheep? It's spring,
and soon they'll be gone above timberline,
climbing to tundra by summer. Some boys
are born to wander, my wife says, but rocky slopes
with spruce and Douglas fir are home.

He tried the navy, the marines, after the army
wouldn't take him, not with a foot like that.
Maybe it's in the genes. I think of wild-eyed years
till I was twenty, and cringe. I loved motorcycles,
too dumb to say no to our son—too many switchbacks
in mountains, too many icy spots in spring.

Doctors stitched back his scalp, hoisted him in traction
like a twisted frame. I sold the motorbike to a junkyard,
but half his foot was gone. Last month, he cashed
his paycheck at the Harley house, roared off
with nothing but a backpack, waving his headband,
leaning into a downhill curve and gone.

Opening the Cabin in March

That's why we're here,
that fish-hook coupling of claws
and bodies tumbling love-locked
down and around between mountains,
bald eagles flicking sparks off

as they fall. Seconds from death,
they flap massive wings
and rise fifty feet and dive
like children climbing a slide.
How many nights on the plains

have we longed to be here
on this rock cliff, stone cabin
balanced on granite,
snowed in on Grandfather's ranch.
Miles across deep valleys,

glaciers crush the boulders.
Sipping cold coffee for hours,
we rock on the deck and stare,
and swear they never move.
Decades since we found this cabin,

backpacking on our honeymoon,
not breathing hard,
able to stand at the ledge
and look down, not even dizzy,
boots new and backpacks snug,

watching for eagles and hawks
across that wide Montana world,
for dish-faced grizzlies
digging out of caves
and swaying in the light.

Ranching at Glacier

Whatever elk sniff, they ignore
for a few more bites of grass,
then twist indignant heads like camels
and waddle off, wagging silver rumps.
Soon they'll climb to summer range

near timberline, except the old
and orphans cougars catch.
We'll drive our cattle out to graze.
We'll turn the hens outside at dawn
to feast on ticks the elk herds shed,

pecking, until coyotes slink back
from town, drawn by our bawling calves,
the cluck and scent of feathers,
wary of our guns but cagey,
pups to raise before the cold.

In Arnold Schwend's Saloon

Plant me down by long-armed soda taps
that don't foam anymore. Arnold Schwend's
Drugstore and Saloon's a gold-bust ghost town
all its own. Four hundred depend on Schwend's

year round for Band-Aids, beer, *The Denver Post*.
He keeps the soda fountain clean for tourists,
serves tea and coffee and two kinds of tap.
His microbrews flare up like dandelions

and blow away. Today's is lager, bittersweet
as licorice. I'm here for our daily cards
as if the store's at stake. Arnold won't bet,
although I always lose. He's older than me

and his daddy's portrait behind the bar, under a lady
not even wearing lace. I watch the eight-foot marvel,
a garish, ripe brunette who hasn't aged
since my young Uncle Walter hauled her up

from Denver, his pin-up girl. A thousand miners
bellied up to the bar and toasted her health
for Uncle Walter in the First World War.
Arnold's father bought my uncle's half of the bar

when Walter shipped out as a corporal to France
and never came back—moose heads and mirror,
spittoons, the Rockies' maja with ribboned wrists
behind her neck, those pink and naughty lips.

Sun Turns the Ice to Oil

Out past the deck, dim light
dazzles the pines, the wet bark
frozen dark. Montana sun
turns ice to oil and crashes
in spangles. High up, cubs bump

and nuzzle slumbering mothers.
Dam bears have heard ice crack
before and pinch back winter
a few more days. They're half
October's size. They'll dig out

hungry and blink at the light
like us, although we're old
and bundled in coats on the deck.
We won't see the bear
but marmots will,

and picas, maybe too late,
caught in the jaws—
their squeals gone hollow,
swallowed or tossed to cubs
learning the taste of blood,

the crash of ice shattering
down slippery slopes,
the delicious comfort of milk
when nursing bears roll
clumsy on their backs.

A Player That Struts and Frets Onstage

The skin remembers its shape for twenty years
and then forgets, needs to be prompted,
rehearsing the same proud lines. At first

a blemish, a wrinkle above the brow.
We say, *Nobody does it better, playing me.*
Around the eyes, crow's feet appear,

puffy lids water pills can't fix. We tug
stretch marks over cheekbones, wondering
what happened here, what prop man

let the makeup dry. Even lavish, two-ton
curtains ravel, have to be clipped
and scrubbed, and raised for the public,

no place to turn but face-lifts,
snips, exotic creams, aging exposed by stiff
gnarled knuckles and liver spots,

less like our hands than our parents'.
Arthritis is a fan that has caught our act
a thousand times, picky about each move

we make onstage, able to spot any change
of pace, the forgotten or lazy line,
demanding the same old, boring bow.

Leaving the Middle Years

A friend asked, "What's your favorite way
to spend a day?" Half wisecrack, I said
Whatever my wife and I are doing.
Easy to say, but true. At our age,
every day is grace and every breath
a blessing. Life is grass, stunningly brief
but abundant in so many ways.

Kids when the President died in 1945,
we had thought what an old, old man he was.
Years ago, watching a documentary
about his life, we realized we were
exactly Roosevelt's age when he died.
That night, we held hands a little longer,
in the dark, with the TV off.

Crows at Dawn in Montana

Two crows make a mockery
of sonnets. I close the book,
stop rocking on the deck, and watch.
They dive, then flap straight up
with peanuts, and the branches bob.

Beaks rip and flip the flimsy shells
and gulp raw peanuts down like pearls.
Some tourist tossed them at dawn
but his car's gone, and he won't mind
if I watch the gobbling act.

The mountain chalet's quiet
except my wife inside, humming,
strumming a comb through her hair.
If Ursula finds more gray
she'll go on humming, knowing it's okay,

our children three thousand miles away
but fine, when they called last night.
She comes outside with coffee,
closing the door so softly
even the crows don't stop.

In Wild Montana Mountains

Hiking this twisting trail, we rest,
heady and sweating by boulders,
dense canopy of fir,
red cedars, tops we can't see.

God knows the number of our days,
how many hairs are left.
We don't keep score. We've lost
too many friends, car wrecks and cancer,

more under sentence of death,
too many codes to count, MS,
ALS, CF. God knows we are dust
and counts our steps,

our days. Too soon, we'll leave
this mountain ranch for home,
down from the hills to the plains.
When our first child arrived

we started the clock—two became three,
soon four and five. Three children
stair-stepped us to middle age
and now we're seventy,

tame in Montana. Even here
in a moss-wet forest of bears,
without a compass or cell phone,
we take one step at a time,

panting and holding hands,
climbing, letting go
to put one palm on a knee
and shove.

When the Days Dwindle Down

Thump of a muscle that wants to be coaxed.
They say to spoil it, jog, start doing sit-ups,
be faithful to diet and calm. Bend down
and touch the toes to keep the old blood pumping.

Cut down on coffee, get lots of sleep.
Before tugging on jogging togs,
my wife and I hold hands on the swing.
An extra hour in the dark

is worth the cold, no smoke in the forest,
a fat crow cawing at dawn, a thousand miles of sky.
We rock and count the last stars backward,
blinking out as we stare, and gone.